A Giant's Giant Pizza

A Play for Young Actors

Julian Garner

A Samuel French Acting Edition

FOUNDED 1830

SAMUELFRENCH-LONDON.CO.UK
SAMUELFRENCH.COM

Copyright © 2001 by Julian Garner
All Rights Reserved

A GIANT'S GIANT PIZZA is fully protected under the copyright laws of the British Commonwealth, including Canada, the United States of America, and all other countries of the Copyright Union. All rights, including professional and amateur stage productions, recitation, lecturing, public reading, motion picture, radio broadcasting, television and the rights of translation into foreign languages are strictly reserved.

ISBN 978-0-573-05126-5

www.samuelfrench-london.co.uk

www.samuelfrench.com

FOR AMATEUR PRODUCTION ENQUIRIES

UNITED KINGDOM AND WORLD EXCLUDING NORTH AMERICA
plays@SamuelFrench-London.co.uk
020 7255 4302/01

Each title is subject to availability from Samuel French,
depending upon country of performance.

CAUTION: Professional and amateur producers are hereby warned that *A GIANT'S GIANT PIZZA* is subject to a licensing fee. Publication of this play does not imply availability for performance. Both amateurs and professionals considering a production are strongly advised to apply to the appropriate agent before starting rehearsals, advertising, or booking a theatre. A licensing fee must be paid whether the title is presented for charity or gain and whether or not admission is charged.

The professional rights in this play are controlled by Judy Daish Associates, 2, St Charles Place, London W10 6EG.

No one shall make any changes in this title for the purpose of production. No part of this book may be reproduced, stored in a retrieval system, or transmitted in any form, by any means, now known or yet to be invented, including mechanical, electronic, photocopying, recording, videotaping, or otherwise, without the prior written permission of the publisher. No one shall upload this title, or part of this title, to any social media websites.

The right of Julian Garner to be identified as author of this work has been asserted by him in accordance with Section 77 of the Copyright, Designs and Patents Act 1988

CHARACTERS
(in order of appearance)

Children (9)
Giant Rumblebottom
Olaf Wiggins
Mum
Dad
Television (1-3)
Nurse
Dr Madcap
Mama Mia
Butler
King
Princess Pauline
Bodyguards (10)

A Giant's Giant Pizza was written for, and first performed by, pupils from Birrallee International School, Trondheim, Norway, in 1998, to mark the school's 25th Anniversary.

Songs

Giant Rumblebottom's Song
Lottery Song
King's Song
Princess Pauline's Song
A Giant's Giant Pizza Rap

Music for the above songs is available on hire from
Samuel French Ltd

FOREWORD

A few years ago I owed my good friend Margot Tønseth a couple of favours. As her school, Birallee International School, in Trondheim, Norway, was coming up to its 25th anniversary, I suggested I might write a play to mark the occasion. Later, realizing just how *many* favours were owed, I offered to direct the production, too. This premièred on 28th April 1998, at Trondheim's Olav's Hall, and was certainly one of the most enjoyable experiences of my twenty-odd years working in the theatre.

Around thirty pupils, aged between 8 and 13, wished to be involved, although levels of ambition varied wildly, from those looking for something to really get their teeth into, to others wanting a walk-on part, and a large group happy to opt for something in between. I did my best to accommodate the full range, though my guiding principle, as writer and director, was that everyone on stage should have a proper part to play, however briefly drawn. So, the number of bodyguards can be adjusted up or down to fit available numbers, although ten is probably the optimum both in terms of comic potential and directorial feasibility; the (optional) prologue was written for a class of eight-year-olds with no previous experience of drama, which was sprung on me after rehearsals had begun. By the same token, a mother's plea that her child be drafted into the production at the eleventh hour, "even if he only plays a stone", was rejected.

Most of the roles are comic, though I've tried to build the dialogue and action such that the comedy arises naturally from playing the scenes as economically as possible. It shouldn't be necessary to graft on great chunks of "comic business" in addition to that described in the stage directions, which has been tried and tested in performance. A second production, which, for example, dispensed with water in the bucket containing Olaf's balaclava, understandably failed to get a laugh when he wrung it out. (The secret is two balaclavas, so that Olaf can change into the dry one after the hospital scene.)

The King is the one character who sees the world from the point of view of a responsible adult, and although it needn't be taken by an older child, it does perhaps require a little more maturity than most of the other roles. Similarly, Giant Rumblebottom needn't be particularly tall—his scale is largely established by the objects he handles—though it might help if the actor/

Foreword

actress can put on a gruff voice! In Trondheim, our giant was played, very successfully, by a girl, and this is one of many roles which can be either cast against gender, or have their gender changed. Dr Madcap began life as a man, but happily survived a sex change, with his madness, if anything, enhanced!

I had the luxury of working with a professional designer and costume supervisor in Trondheim, which proved a boon to every aspect of the production. The action of the play needs to move swiftly between a number of different locations—Giant Rumblebottom's castle, the Wiggins's living room, the hospital, the Royal Palace, Mama Mia's pizzeria, etc. It's important to avoid all but the briefest scene changes in order to keep the story flowing and avoid energy drops, but I wanted the different locations to be visually differentiated. Hanne Horte came up with the brilliantly simple solution of including set elements into the costumes of key characters. So, the hospital is represented as a large cut-out Donald McGill-like nurse, with holes for the actress's face and arms. Similarly, the Butler comes complete with a cut-out palace, and Mama Mia is incorporated into her pizzeria. The performers also wear conventional costumes, allowing them to emerge from behind their free-standing set elements as required by the action of the scenes. Another effective design solution was to keep the sofa from the Wiggins's living room (Scene 2) in place for the subsequent scenes, covering it first with a white sheet for the hospital, then something suitably regal for the scene at the Royal Palace. Otherwise, apart from a little Italianate table and chairs for the pizzeria and a small raised platform from which the King, and Olaf, address the nation, we banished all furniture from the stage, working on the theory that it is best to keep young, inexperienced actors on their feet. A huge foam rubber pizza slice set the scene inside Rumblebottom's castle. Otherwise, there were a few hand-props, the actors and nothing else.

The general setting was established by Hanne's beautiful backdrop, which consisted of a line-drawn illustration of all the story's different locations, dominated by the giant's brooding, mountain-top castle. When lit from behind, the illustration gave way to the towering silhouette of Giant Rumblebottom himself, the spectacular effect of his shrinking was achieved simply by having him walk slowly forward from the light source towards the backdrop. The backdrop also happily dispensed with the need for complicated lighting. A bit of front lighting, literally to illuminate the stage, and a few shadowy gobos to establish the atmosphere of the giant's castle, was all that was required to render the show adequately "theatrical".

Simplicity was the watchword for music and sound cues, also. As the auditorium was quite large, we did provide a microphone for the singers, but there were few other concessions to technology. I'd composed the music on

A Giant's Giant Pizza

guitar, and we decided not to retexture the sound, i.e. through a synthesizer. For the rap, our MD tapped out the appropriate rhythm on the soundbox of his guitar. He also covered scene changes, such as they were, with sharp taps on a wood-block, which effectively kept the audience focused on the stage. The only pre-recorded sound cues were: a flushing toilet, for the punchline of the Princess's song in the loo (the joke wouldn't work as well without it), the sound of helicopters when the pizza is parachuted in for Rumblebottom (which helps maintain the illusion of scale), and the distant explosion at the end of the play which signifies the success of Olaf's plan.

Olaf's ears were initially a problem. Although visually perfect, the latex joke-shop monstrosities kept falling off, especially when he put on or took off the balaclava. The solution was to sew the ears on to a narrow hair-band, which was further secured under the chin with a piece of flesh-coloured elastic. Otherwise, all props, furniture, effects and even stage business not essential to the action were vigorously excised. We used a token amount of make-up (not essential); costumes were simple and purposefully child-like, the bodyguards provided their own hilarious armoury of plant-douches, catapults fly-swats and kitchen utensils, and our costume supervisor, Anne Spetz, fresh off the plane from the fashion industry in Milan, could make a plastic bag look stylish.

I worried that the children might find the song lyrics difficult to learn—not least the rap; with only one or two exceptions, the entire cast was performing in their second language—English. In the event, our prompter remained unemployed throughout the four performance run. There were no technical hiccups (there being almost no technicals to hiccup) and we turned in a forty-five minute show stuffed with laughs and even a few thrills. Audiences literally gasped as Giant Rumblebottom shrank before their very eyes!

A Giant's Giant Pizza began life as an impromptu bedtime story for my daughters, Leoni and Natali, which we then acted out, on video, in my mother's garden in England during the summer of 1997. From this prototype I fashioned a rehearsal script which, with minor refinements, is the one printed here. The play is dedicated, then, to Margot Tønseth, who weathered a good deal of opposition to make the play happen, to Leoni and Natali, who provided many of the better ideas, and, not least, to the wonderful cast and crew of the first production. Many thanks to all and sundry.

Julian Garner

PRODUCTION NOTES

Giant Rumblebottom's shadow is created by placing a light source several metres behind the backdrop screen. The actor playing Rumblebottom then stands between the light source and the screen. The closer the actor stands to the light source the larger the shadow projected on to the screen will be. Allow plenty of time to experiment with this effect; its success will ensure a vivid and genuinely scary giant.

The play is written to move swiftly and easily from one scene to the next: settings and costumes should therefore be minimal.

A GIANT'S GIANT PIZZA

PROLOGUE

Children enter, variously

First Child The giant trod on our house!
Second Child He trod on ours, too!
Third Child And ours!
Fourth Child And ours!
Fifth Child *And* ours!
Sixth Child And *ours*!
Seventh Child He trod on our whole farm!
Eighth Child The buildings are flattened!
Seventh Child The animals are all dead or run away!
Sixth Child Why can't he look where he's going?
Fifth Child He wasn't wearing his glasses.
Fourth Child He never does!
Ninth Child He can't see all the way from his head to his toes, it's miles.
Sixth Child That's no excuse!
Third Child It's getting dark.
Second Child It's cold.
Fifth Child Where are we going to sleep tonight?
Eighth child I want my mummy!

Pause

Ninth Child (*pointing*) What's that thing over there?
Sixth Child (*investigating*) I think it's one of the giant's handkerchiefs.

Others utter cries of "Ugh!", "Poo!", "Disgusting!"

Fourth Child Oh dear, it's starting to snow!

Pause

Ninth Child We'll have to make a tent.

S/he and three others take the handkerchief by the corners and stretch it out. The other children crawl underneath

First Child I'm not sleeping in there! It's not even a clean handkerchief.
Ninth Child Then you'll freeze to death.

All except the First Child huddle together beneath the giant's handkerchief. They begin singing a lullaby

First Child Oh! Look there!

Emerging from beneath the handkerchief, the others wonder "What?", "What is it?", "What's the matter?"

I saw a shooting star!
Third Child Did you make a wish?
First Child Of course I did.
Sixth Child Don't tell us what it was, or it won't come true!

All except the First Child go back under the handkerchief. They sing a lullaby

First Child (*to the audience*) I wished that someone big and strong and brave would come and destroy the giant.
Ninth Child (*popping her head out*) Come in out of the snow or you will freeze to death!

The First Child joins the others. They finish singing the lullaby

The Children exit

SCENE 1

Giant Rumblebottom enters, breathless, carrying a sack

Giant My name's Rumblebottom, but I'm a giant, so don't laugh or I might pick you up between my finger and thumb and eat you—like this! (*He takes a cow out of his sack*) Mmmmm, I'm starving!
Cow Moooo! Moooooo!
Giant (*regarding the cow for a moment then tossing it back in the sack*) Actually, I can't stand raw animals, all those horns and feathers and teeth and hair—yuk! (*Annoyed*) It's always the same—I go down to the valley and get lots of fat juicy beasts for my dinner but by the time I've dragged them all the way up the mountain to my castle I'm too puffed out and sweaty to cook them! (*He remembers something*) Where did I put that car-thingy? (*He brings a small car out of the sack and examines it from all*

Scene 1

sides) I found it in the valley—they've all got them down there. From now on, when I go down to get myself some food, I'll just bung it in the boot and drive home! Hmmm. It's a bit small. (*He tries to get into the car*) How are you supposed to...? (*He realizes it's useless*) I WANT PIZZA! (*He takes a mobile phone from the sack and dials a number*) Give me the King! I don't care if he is in an important meeting, this is Giant Rumblebottom and in case you don't know it—

Song: Giant Rumblebottom's Song
I'm as tall as the post office tower
I eat thirty-five cows in an hour
When I want something done
I expect folk to run
'Cause they know I'm the one with the power.

I'm lazy, I admit, and I'm greedy
I've never once given to the needy
I couldn't care less
For people's happiness
'Cause people are pathetic and weedy.

I'm a giant and giants are tough
And giants just can't get enough
If a giant wants a thing
He just phones up the King
And the monarch procures him the stuff.

I want a million big pizzas for lunch
With wafer thin bases that crunch
Topped with mushrooms and cheese
And pepperoni, please,
You'll deliver them soon I've a hunch.

If you don't, you know what I'll do
I'll destroy your whole kingdom for you!
I'll behave like a lout
And blunder about
And cause a disaster or two!

Giant Rumblebottom exits

SCENE 2

Olaf's house. There is a sofa and a television set with an actor inside it as the announcer

Olaf enters, with his hands over his huge ears. He searches about for something in vain. He calls off

Olaf Mum! Dad! Have either of you seen my balaclava?
Dad (*off*) It's by the TV. I used it to dust the furniture with!
Olaf Dust the *furniture*…?!
Mum (*off*) No, no, it's on the tea tray—I used it to strain the coffee with!
Olaf Strain the *coffee*…?!
Dad (*off*) Oh, no, I remember now… Olaf, your balaclava's in the bucket—I used it to wash the floor with!
Olaf The *bucket*…? The *floor*…?! My *balaclava*! (*He fishes a soaking wet balaclava out of a bucket, wrings it out and puts it on, making sure it covers his ears. He takes a mobile phone from his pocket and dials*) Hello, is that the Royal Palace?… Er, my name's Olaf. Can I speak to Princess Pauline, please? I'm in her class at school and I need to ask her a question about homework.… Thanks, I'll wait. (*To the audience*) She won't want to talk to me, she's so cool and gorgeous and I'm so ugly. She never speaks to me at school, even though we're in the same group for Dinosaurs. She probably thinks I look like a tetradactyl, with these ears. Who do I think I'm kidding? I'm just wasting my time. I might as well put the phone down… (*Into the phone*) He-hello, Princess? High there, your Lowness, so pool of you to foam at the… I mean, so cool of you to come to the…

Mum rushes in with her Lottery tickets

Mum Quick! It's the Lottery! (*To Olaf*) Olaf, get off the phone, why haven't you switched on the telly, it's seven o'clock!
Olaf Sorry, can't talk now. (*He puts the phone away*)
Mum (*calling off*) Reg, bring your coupons!

Olaf switches on the television

Dad rushes in with his coupons

Dad It's a Double Draw!
Mum It's starting!

Olaf takes out his Lottery tickets. They all stare at the screen

Scene 2

Television 1 And now for the Lottery Draw! Remember, there's a Double Draw today and you could win a massive three million pounds!
Dad I'm feeling lucky!
Mum Shh!
Television 1 And the numbers are—two and one, twenty-one. One seven, number seventeen. Six and four, sixty-four. All the fives, fifty-five. Eight and nine, eighty-nine. Seven and eight, seventy-eight. And, the final number tonight is ... fourteen!
Dad I got four right!
Mum What?
Dad I got four right!
Mum That means you've won something!
Television 1 With seven correct numbers you win three million pounds! With six correct numbers you win fifteen thousand eight hundred and fifteen pounds. Five correct numbers wins you one hundred and forty-six pounds. And, finally, with four correct numbers tonight, you win...
Dad Six pounds eighty-three pence! Yes!
Television 1 And now, straight on to our second draw...

Only Olaf follows the second draw, the sound of which is drowned out by Mum and Dad's song and dance

Song: Lottery Song

Dad	I just won the lottery
Mum	Six whole pounds and eighty-three
Dad	Never ever thought it would happen to me
Mum	He's pretty happy, that's easy to see
Dad	I feel as rich as a Devon Cream Tea
Mum	With all of six pounds eighty-three?
	Open yourself an investment account!
Dad	It's winning that's exciting, not the amount.
	Oh, you feel so great when you win a few quid
	You can dance and sing, really flip your lid
	'Cause the Finger of Fate has picked you out
	And the voice of God has proclaimed with a shout
	That you're an individual amongst the crowd
	You can stand up straight, feel tall and proud

Olaf Mum, Dad!
Mum You're not nothing, you're alive and kicking
The fruits of life are yours for the picking!
Olaf On the second draw I won...
Mum Not now, your father's celebrating! (*To Dad*) We'll pop a bottle of bubbly in the kitchen!

Mum and Dad exit

Olaf (*stunned*) ...three million pounds?

Mum enters

Mum And take that balaclava off, you look deranged!

Mum exits

Olaf I can't believe it!
Television 1 Mirror, mirror on the wall, who is the fairest of them all?

Television 2 and Television 3 enter

Television 2 Not you, that's for sure! Is that a nose or the winning entry for the World's Longest Cucumber Competition? I'm sorry, are those ears, or are you getting ready for take off? Oh, you're a *person*—silly me, I thought you were the side of a house! Or the back of a bus!
Television 1 Boohoohoo!
Television 3 Does your appearance let you down?
Olaf And how!
Television 3 Don't despair! Now, thanks to the miracles of cosmetic surgery, your body need never cause you grief again! Just call the New You Helpline and our experts will advise you on how best to rearrange your attributes. And remember—You Too Can Have a Brand New You! Noses, ears and saggy bottoms our speciality. Phone now on 0800 007008.
Olaf (*whipping out his mobile, dialling*) Hello, my name is Olaf Wiggins, I just won three million pounds on the Lottery. How soon would you be able to fix my ears?

A Nurse comes in, immediately

Wow—that soon, huh?

The Televisions exit

Scene 3

The Hospital. The sofa is covered with a white sheet

Nurse If you'd like to take a seat, Dr Madcap will be with you directly. Shall I take your balaclava?

Scene 3

Olaf No, thanks. We go back a long way. There are no secrets between us.
Nurse (*after a slight pause*) I see.

Dr Madcap enters

Dr Madcap OK, OK, I'm a busy woman, who's next, is this the guy? What seems to be the problem, sir? Is it your heart, is it your head, is it your stomach?

The Nurse whispers in Dr Madcap's ear

Oh, so you don't like your ears, huh? So, what, you want more of them or do you want less?
Olaf They make me feel awkward and silly. I feel everyone's laughing at me behind my back.
Dr Madcap I understand perfectly. What say we take a look-see? (*She removes Olaf's balaclava. She roars with laughter at the sight of his ears and stops abruptly*) OK, sonny, so what size do you want these dishes of yours?
Olaf Normal sized.
Dr Madcap Normal for humans, I take it? For elephants they're normal already! (*She roars with laughter again and stops abruptly*) Nurse, prepare my instruments—I'll operate immediately.

The Nurse hands her a wood-saw

OK, sonny, keep still, and remember—this is going to hurt you a lot more than it hurts me!
Olaf Wait! Aren't you going to give me an injection first?
Dr Madcap An injection?
Olaf An anaesthetic—it'll be painful, otherwise!
Dr Madcap (*after a slight pause*) I see. Sorry, sir, a little misunderstanding there. Nurse, the patient would prefer the pain*less* treatment.
Nurse Yes, Doctor.

The Nurse goes out

Olaf Is she going to give me an injection?
Dr Madcap No, she's going to give you an application.

The Nurse comes in shaking a canister of shaving foam

This is how it works. First, the Nurse—an *expert* in her field—applies some Specially Formulated Fast-Acting Reducing Foam to your offending extremities.

The Nurse squirts foam on to Olaf's ears

Olaf Hey!
Dr Madcap Then, you pay your bill. (*She presents Olaf with a bill*) Plastic's fine, cash preferred.
Olaf Seven hundred thousand pounds?!
Nurse Our special rate for Lottery winners.
Dr Madcap Our *very* special rate for Lottery winners.

Olaf takes out a wad of money. Dr Madcap snatches it

Bingo!

Dr Madcap rushes out of the room

Nurse You can go now. Just wash the foam off in half an hour and your ears will be just perfect.
Olaf Is that all? A couple of squirts of foam? For seven hundred thousand pounds?
Nurse Dr Madcap is an expert in her field.
Olaf What field's that—daylight robbery?

The Nurse exits, miffed

Oh, well. At least I can phone the Princess in— (*he looks at his watch*) twenty-nine minutes and thirty-six seconds, precisely! (*He notices the canister of foam and picks it up*) This might come in useful. OK—show me to a phone, Tone!

Olaf exits

Scene 4

The Palace

A phone rings

A Butler enters and takes a mobile phone out of his pocket

The King runs in

Scene 4

King Don't answer that! It's almost certainly Giant Rumblebottom with more of his impossible demands. Oh, my God—he's ruining the country! What with all the compensation I have to pay to everyone he steals food from, there's no more money left! My army consists of ten men with catapults, my navy's a leaky rowing boat with one oar, and my air force is a fleet of paper gliders with the words "Very Dangerous Fighter Aircraft" written on then!

The phone keeps ringing

Oh, for God's sake! (*He snatches the phone from the Butler. Into the phone*) It's no good, Rumblebottom, you can't *have* any more—you've bled us dry—it's over—we're finished—go rob and pillage some other country! What did we ever do to you, you great fat booby?! ... Who is this? ... Olaf? Olaf who? ... Er, yes, she's here somewhere... Pauline! (*To the Butler*) Have you seen the Princess?

Butler The last I heard she was practising on her drum kit, Your Highness.

The Princess enters, reading a comic. She finishes her page before speaking

Princess You called, Daddy-o?
King There's someone on the phone for you. Olaf somebody-or-other...
Princess Olaf! Oh my God! How do I look? Is my hair OK? How's my mascara? Have I got time to change my outfit? Oh, jeepers creepers, *Olaf*?!

The King thrusts the phone into her hand. She adopts a "cool" tone

Hi, Olaf, how's tricks? ... (*Excited*) Would I like to go out for a pizza, with *you*? (*Silently, triumphant*) Yes! (*Cool again*) Sounds cool to me. Why don't I meet you at the Palace of Pizza in (*she looks at her watch*) half an hour? Be there or be square.

The Butler takes the phone from her

Yahoo!
King Good news, my dear? Giant Rumblebottom's gone down with typhoid?
Princess Oh, much more sensational than that! Olaf Wiggins has asked me out on a date!
King Olaf Wiggins?
Princess He's this guy in my class. He has the cutest ears you ever did see! Though you don't see them often, he hides them under this stupid hat all the time. But maybe he only wears that at school? Oh my God, I hope so!

I'm meeting him in town in twenty-eight minutes and thirty-two seconds, precisely, so I don't have a moment to spare!
King An evening out will do you the world of good, I'm sure. Butler—summon the Princess's bodyguards.
Butler Will ten be sufficient, Your Majesty?
King I suppose so...
Princess Ten bodyguards?!

The Butler exits

What kind of a date is *that* going to be?
King I'm sorry, my dear, but I can't take the risk. Giant Rumblebottom may try to snatch you.
Princess But Dad...!
King No buts! If Rumblebottom gets hold of you I'd never forgive myself. The very thought of it makes me shudder violently! (*He does so*)
Head Bodyguard (*off*) Bodyguards, by the left quick *march*!
Bodyguards (*off*) Left... Left... Left, right, left... Left... Left... Left, right, left, right, left... Left!

The Bodyguards march on, all ten of them wearing shades and dark suits

Head Bodyguard Company halt!

They halt

Princess's Bodyguards reporting for duty, sir!
King The Princess is meeting one of her chums for a jolly evening out in town. Stick to her like limpets! Like glue, you understand! Though I want you to be discreet about it, too.
Bodyguards Discreet's our middle name, Boss!
Head Bodyguard Surround her!

They surround the Princess completely

King Have a nice time, dear.
Princess Yeah, sure, Dad.
Head Bodyguard Company, by the left, discreet *stroll*!

The Bodyguards shuffle off, whistling nonchalantly, with the Princess
    Song: King's Song
King (*singing*) I hate being King of this country
    The job is a right royal pain
    In fact if it wasn't for Pauline

I'd probably move to Spain
And live the life of Reilly
On a nice hot sandy beach...

But what would Pauline think of her dad
If he bunked off abroad like an apple gone bad
And left the nation to a Giant's whim?
If only I could get the better of him!
I've drawn up plans and commissioned reports
Held a summit conference at a holiday resort
Made secret pacts with a dozen foreign powers
Had big walls built with fortified towers.
But what can you do about a foe so tall
That he just steps over your highest wall
And flattens your armies with the palm of his hand?
It's a bit of a problem, you'll understand.

I love being Dad to my daughter
It's the one thing that keeps me sane
That and the thought of a future
When she might feel safe again.
I can't see how it'll happen
Though I pray for it every night...

Never say die, it's an easy thing to say
If you never have a care or a worry all day!
Till the Giant came along my life was great!
I do hope Pauline doesn't stay out late!

The King exits

SCENE 5

The Palace of Pizza

Olaf, waiting outside the Palace of Pizza, is wearing his balaclava

Bodyguards (*off; approaching*) Left! Left! Left, right, left! Left! Left! Left, right, left, right, left! Left!

The Bodyguards march on with the Princess

Head Bodyguard Bodyguards, *halt!*

They stop

    Stand at ease! Stand easy.
Princess Oh, very discreet, guys.
Olaf Princess Pauline?
Princess Olaf! Hi. I didn't notice you out there. Come and join me.
Olaf How about I order some pizza, first?
Princess Hey, that'd be cool! Mine's an American Way. Dudes—what're you having?

The Bodyguards simultaneously call out "American Way", "O Solo Mio", "Vegetable Garden", "Sea Food Special", etc.

    Stop, stop, *stop*! American Way *all* the way, I think, Olaf. Put it on the Royal Bill.
Olaf No way, Jose! This is my treat. I just won first prize on the Lottery!
Princess You did?
Olaf Three million portraits of the King!
Princess Cool. As. A. *Pool*!

Olaf rings a bell

Mama Mia appears

Mama Mia What-a you a-want?
Olaf American Way to the power of ten, please!
Mama Mia No-a pizza tonight!
Olaf No-a pizza…?! But this is the *Palace* of Pizza!
Mama Mia The Giant he-a take all-a we a-bake! That big-a fat-a booby, he-a eat-a them-a all, every a-one! Six a-hundred and a-ten so far tonight, and the night it is a-still a-young! Mama Mia!

Mama Mia exits

Olaf What shall we do?
Princess Let's sit down and make a plan.

The Bodyguards make it impossible for her to sit

    Guys, this is hopeless! I'm giving you the evening off!
Bodyguards No can do, Your Highness. Our orders are "Stick to the Princess like glue!" And the Princess, that's you, Princess.
Princess Oh, I'm beginning to wish that old Giant *would* kidnap me! At least it would be something *happening*! I spend my whole life wrapped in cotton

wool—it's so un*cool*! I'm not allowed to do anything on my own except go to the toilet. Well, that's what I'm going to do right now!

The Bodyguards shuffle with her over to the toilet, marked "Ladies"

Sorry, guys, ladies only. Don't worry: I promise not to flush myself down the pan!
Bodyguards Hahaha! She's got a sense of humour, that Princess, hahaha.

The Princess goes in

Princess (*off; singing*) I'm singing in the loo
    Just singing in the loo
    I must have a wee and I might need a pooh
    Tum tumti tum
    Di di diddly do
    Just singing and dancing in the...

Toilet flush followed by a long silence. The Bodyguards become uneasy

Bodyguards Princess! Are you all right? Princess Pauline? Princess? Wah! She's flushed herself down the toilet!

The Bodyguards all rush inside

The Princess nips out from behind the door, slams it shut and wedges it with a stick

(*Off*) Princess? Princess? Help! She's tricked us! Let us out! Princess! Help! You can't do this to us! Princess!
Princess (*to Olaf*) Nice dudes—but not the brightest. So—where shall we go?
Olaf Anywhere you like—you're looking at the winner of three million smackeroos, remember?!
Princess Any chance of looking at a bit more of you, Olaf? Your ears, for example?
Olaf My ears?
Princess They're the *cutest*! Why do you hide them behind that stupid balaclava all the time?
Olaf You *like* my ears?
Princess Every square inch of them!
Bodyguards (*off*) Princess! Princess! Let us out of here!
Olaf Let's go get ourselves some pizza!

Princess Well, there's only one place we'll get any of *that* tonight. Follow me.

The Princess and Olaf run out

Bodyguards (*off*) His Royal Bossness ain't gonna like this, Princess! Princess!!

SCENE 6

Sound of a helicopter approaching. A small parachute with a box attached falls to the stage. The helicopter recedes

Giant Rumblebottom comes on

He detaches the box from the parachute. He takes a miniature pizza about the size of a two pound piece from the box and holds it up

Giant To a human being this is a very, very large pizza indeed. In fact, they call it—haha—a *giant* pizza! I have to eat ten of these things at a time just to feel I've got something in my mouth! What I want is a *giant's* giant pizza—these things are such hard work! I'm going to take a nap and then, when I wake up, I'll work out some way to force that useless, no-good King to give me satisfaction!

The Giant goes out

He is soon heard snoring, loudly, off (i.e. amplified)

The Princess enters with a pizza the size of a wheel

Princess So—is this a pizza, or what?

Olaf follows her in

Olaf It's madness, is what it is!
Princess Yeah, but fun too, huh? Did you see the videos he had in there? *The Lost World, Independence Day, The Spice Girls Video...*
Olaf He's asleep on the sofa in there!
Princess So, you want to wake him—this isn't exciting enough for you? Stop whiffling, Olaf, and have some pizza. And how about taking your balaclava off and showing the world your wonderful ears?
Olaf I can't.

Scene 6 15

Princess Why not?
Olaf I... I haven't washed them today.
Princess What's a little dirt when it's someone you love?
Olaf I... I have an ear infection, you might catch it.
Princess If it's yours, I want to!
Olaf Erm ... er... My dad spilt—what's your least favourite colour?
Princess Blue.
Olaf ...Blue paint all over them and it won't come off.
Princess Oh, *least* favourite? That's yellow; blue's my *favourite* colour.
Olaf I meant yellow! All over my ears—yuk!
Princess I won't look, I can just *feel* them!
Olaf (*desperate*) Why do you like my ears?
Princess Because ... they're part of what makes you *you*. No-one else has ears like yours. They're unique.
Olaf The rest of me is unique, too!
Princess Olaf, why are you making such a fuss?
Olaf Because ... because...

The Giant suddenly gives a loud snort in his sleep, making them both jump. He's soon snoring evenly again

(*Whispering*) Because I hate the giant!
Princess I hate him, too.
Olaf Maybe we could get rid of him?
Princess Get rid of the giant? Now, that *would* be cool.
Olaf I have a plan!
Princess Ooo, you make it sound so exciting, Olaf!
Olaf First, we creep into the video room and then, whilst he's asleep, we cover him all over with some Specially Formulated Fast-Acting Reducing Foam. Then we wait for the foam to shrink him to the size of a mouse. Then put him in a box and take him down to your father, who throws him into the deepest, darkest dungeon and throws away the key. And then everyone lives happily ever after!
Princess That's a great plan, Olaf!
Olaf You think so?
Princess It's a plan from Plan Land!
Olaf Well, you know, it's just a plan...
Princess There's just one thing about this plan, Olaf.
Olaf What's that?
Princess Specially Formulated Fast-Acting Reducing Foam—do we happen to have any of this stuff to hand at this precise moment in time?
Olaf Only ten cans— (*he gives her one from his rucksack*) but it should be enough if we use it sparingly.
Princess (*amazed*) Where did you get that?

Olaf (*taking out another can*) It's a long story, but we've no time to lose—we've got a real chance to rid the country of the curse of the Giant, but Rumblebottom might wake up any moment! You start at his head and I'll start at his toes!
Princess Wow—this is something *really* happening!

The Giant's huge shadow appears on the back wall, dwarfing Olaf and the Princess

There's a hissing sound as they mime covering the sleeping Rumblebottom with foam. Then they come downstage and watch as, miraculously, the Giant shrinks before their eyes

Olaf It's working!
Princess This isn't just cool, it's deep frozen, man! I mean, like, liquid nitrogen!
Olaf Yeah—Strontium 90!
Princess Actually, that's *heavy*, not cool.
Olaf Oh.

The Giant shrinks to next to nothing (See Production Notes)

Olaf rushes out

Princess Olaf, what are you doing!
Olaf (*off*) Got you!
Giant (*in a high, squeaky voice*) Help! Help!

Olaf comes in with the Giant held in his hands like a beetle

Princess Yeah!

The Princess runs out, and comes back immediately with a pizza box

Put him in here!

Olaf does so

Giant's Voice Help! Help! Let me out of here!
Princess We've got you now, you great big bully!
Olaf Minuscule *little* bully!
Giant's Voice Let me out, you foul brats! You'll pay for this!
Olaf (*rapping on the box*) One more word from you, Giant Rumblebottom——

Princess Midget Squeakybum!
Olaf —And we'll feed you to the cat!
Princess Miaow! (*She shakes the box and throws it to Olaf*)

Olaf shakes it and throws it back. The Giant squeaks with rage as they send the box back and forth. Finally, Olaf puts it on the floor and places something heavy on the lid

But hey, it's dark outside. We can't go down the mountain, now, we'd get lost.
Olaf We'll go down first thing in the morning. In the meantime, let's go and eat some more pizza and watch some of the giant's cool videos.
Princess Olaf, this is the best night of my entire life! Can you imagine the look on my father's face when we show him Giant Rumblebottom in a box?!

They go out

Scene 7

The Palace

The King and the Bodyguards enter

The King glares at the shame-faced Bodyguards

King Call yourself bodyguards? Body *odours* more like!
Bodyguards Sorry, Your Bossness. We didn't mean to let her get away...
King One more word and I'll have you making an attempt at the World Bungee Jumping Record, only WITHOUT A BUNGEE! Is that understood?!

The Bodyguards clamp their hands over their mouths

The Butler enters

Butler Olaf's Mum and Dad, Your Majesty.

Dad enters, followed by Mum

Dad Where is he? Where's our Olaf——
Mum —and his three million pounds Lottery winnings?
Dad We know he's here! He keeps ringing this number, and we found a

whole exercise book of poems about your daughter in his bedroom. Where is he——

Mum —and his Lottery winnings?

Dad There's a law against this sort of thing.

Butler Please it Sir and Madam to know that they are in the presence of his Royal Majesty the King, First Officer of His Royal Armed Forces, Head of the Church...

Dad Don't try and impress us with all that Royal nonsense. We pay our taxes, we know our rights! If he wants our respect he's got to *earn* it. And the first thing he can do is hand over our son——

Mum —and his Lottery winnings.

Dad Our little boy, the light of our life, the love of our heart, our precious little diddums——

Mum —who hit the jackpot on the Lottery...

Dad WHERE IS HE?!

King (*to Bodyguards*) Would you care to tell these good people where their son is?

The Bodyguards shuffle about, awkwardly

Tell them!

Bodyguards In the castle of Giant Rumblebottom.

Dad WHAT?!

Bodyguards (*louder*) In the castle of Giant...

Mum faints into Dad's arms

Dad Oh my God!

King (*indicating the Bodyguards to the Butler*) I want you to take these imbeciles away and shoot them.

Butler Yes, Your Majesty.

King And then I want you to chop their heads off and sew them back on again. And then I want you to hang, draw and quarter them, then stick them back together again. And then I want you to drag them behind a chariot for three days and nights without stopping. And then I want you to give them a thousand lashes each. And then I want you to boil them all in oil. And then I want you to feed them to the lions. And *then*, I want you to SEND THEM TO BED WITHOUT ANY TEA!

Bodyguards (*begging on their knees*) Oh no, Boss, please, not without our tea! Please, please! We promise we won't do it again!

King Take them away!

The Butler herds out the Bodyguards

Dad You'll have to go up there after him! Send in the army, the navy, the air force!
King Armed with catapults and paper darts?
Dad You must give Rumblebottom whatever he demands! It doesn't matter what it is, we've got to have our little Olaf back!
Mum (*recovering*) And his Lottery winnings.
King Sir, we don't know yet, that he *has* got them.
Dad Huh?
King For all we know, *they* might have got *him*. I wouldn't put anything past *my* child. And now, if you will excuse me, I have a country to run.

The King exits, grandly

Scene 8

The Giant's video room

Olaf and the Princess are asleep

A cockerel crows outside. The Princess wakes. She regards the sleeping Olaf, fondly. Very gently removes his balaclava. His ears are as big as at the start of the play but the Princess hasn't seen them any other way so she doesn't think it odd

Princess Wow!

Olaf wakes up

Olaf (*realizing his balaclava has been removed*) Wah! (*He clamps his hands to his ears, feels that they have grown large again*) Wah!
Princess They are the most brilliant ears I ever saw. And to think that you love me! What have I done to be so lucky?

          Song: Princess Pauline's Song
    Olaf, some girls fall in love
    With pictures in a magazine
    They buy all the latest CDs
    Of the lover of their dreams
    They take in all the movies
    Buy all the merchandise
    And moon around each playtime
    With that love-look in their eyes.

But Olaf for me there's you
And Olaf for me you'll do
Yes Olaf for me there's you
And I hope that will always be true.

At school I sit behind you
So I can watch you secretly
And it gives me such a thrill
When I think you might be watching me
I don't know how it happened
That I started loving you
But when you phoned and asked me out tonight
It was a dream come true.

Because Olaf for me there's you
And Olaf for me you'll do
Yes Olaf for me there's you
And I hope that will always be true. (*Repeat*)

Olaf Oh, no!
Princess What is it, Olaf?
Olaf If my ears... Then, the Giant... Oh my God!
Princess What? What is it?

Olaf rushes out and returns immediately with the pizza box, which has burst

Olaf The Giant's grown big again!
Princess Olaf, will you stop talking in riddles for a moment and kindly explain yourself?
Olaf The foam—I took it from the hospital—I left a cheque—they put it on my ears to make them smaller...
Princess The cheque?
Olaf The *foam*! But it doesn't work properly, it wears off! First, my ears—and now, the Giant...

Giant Rumblebottom's shadow appears on the back wall—he's huge again

Giant (*amplified*) FI, FY, FO, FESS, I SMELL THE BLOOD OF A YOUNG PRINCESS!
Princess (*angrily*) I'm going to bite him! (*She runs behind the screen*)
Olaf Princess! Don't! Princess!
Princess (*her shadow appears next to that of the Giant*) Die, Rumblebottom! (*She tries to bite him*)

Scene 9

The Giant grabs her. She screams

Olaf Pauline!
Giant AND NOW I'VE GOT *YOU*, MY LITTLE BEAUTY! LET'S SEE WHAT YOUR STUPID FATHER, THE KING, HAS TO SAY *NOW*, SHALL WE?!
Princess Run, Olaf!
Olaf Don't worry, Pauline, I'll get help!

Olaf runs out

Giant HELP? FROM WHOM? NO-ONE CAN HELP YOU NOW, PRINCESS! NO-ONE!

His cruel laugh echoes as the shadow fades

Scene 9

The Butler, Bodyguards, Mama Mia, Dr Madcap and the Nurse, Olaf's Mum and Dad, the Children all watching television

Television His Royal Highness, The King, will address the nation.

The King enters

The Television is held up in front of him

King I have just received a telephone call from the Giant Rumblebottom, who informs me that he has my daughter, the Princess Pauline, captive in his castle.
Dad What about our Olaf——
Mum —and his millions?
Everyone Else Shhhhh!
Mum (*shaking her handbag at them*) Shhhh yourself!
King The giant is prepared to release the Princess on one condition only. Namely, the delivery, by midday tomorrow, of a pizza.
Mum A *pizza*?

Everybody laughs

King But this is no ordinary pizza. In Rumblebottom's own words, it must be "a *giant's* giant pizza"; the size of a skating rink, topped with a hundred

kilos of pepperoni, a hundred kilos of cheese, a field of mushrooms and onions, a tropical island of pineapple, all floating on a lake of tomato sauce.
Mum Why is he telling *us* this?
Most of the Others Shhhh!
Mum Shhh yourself! (*She attacks people with her handbag*)

Dad drags her back

King Obviously, such a pizza will be very, very expensive to make. And the fact is that the Royal Treasury doesn't have enough money in it to foot the bill.
Dr Madcap He wants *us* to pay for it!
Nurse Outrageous!
Dr Madcap He makes a mess of running the country so *we* have to pay the price!
Nurse Shocking!
Dad Typical!
Mama Mia We should do it for the sake of the Princess!
Bodyguards Yes!
Mum Why should *we* be responsible for his mistakes?
Dr Madcap Hear, hear!
King The truth is, my good people, that I have paid so much in compensation to victims of the Giant's past actions that I am now bankrupt. Not just the treasury, but my own private accounts are all empty.
Dad Sell the Crown Jewels!
King The Crown Jewels were sold a long time ago...
Dr Madcap Let out the palace!
King Last year the Royal Palace was sold to a business consortium, who plan to turn it into a theme park...
Dad You should have got rid of the Giant sooner, shouldn't you!
Nurse Not our fault!
Mum We're not paying!
Mama Mia Anything to save-a the Princess!
Dr Madcap Never!
Butler Yes!
Mum/Dad/Nurse/Dr Madcap No!
Butler/Bodyguards/Mama Mia Yes!
Mum/Dad/Nurse/Dr Madcap No!
Butler/Bodyguards/Mama Mia Yes!
Mum/Dad/Nurse/Dr Madcap No!
Butler/Bodyguards/Mama Mia Yes, yes, yes, yes, yes, yes, yes... (*Etc.*)
Mum/Dad/Nurse/Dr Madcap (*overlapping*) No, no, no, no, no, no, no, no, no, no, no... (*Etc.*)

Scene 9

King And so, my people, it is with a heavy heart that I appeal to you, for the sake of my beloved daughter the Princess, to help me in my hour of need…
Dad What about our Olaf——
Mum —and his millions?!
Dad The Giant's got him, too!
Olaf (*off*) No, he hasn't!
Dad Olaf?!
Mum Our money!

Olaf rushes in, breathless, not wearing a balaclava

Dad You got away?!
Mum Have you got the money with you? Can we see it?
Olaf Later. First, I must speak to the King! Take me to the King, it's urgent!
King (*coming out from behind the television*) What is it?
Olaf Your Majesty—everybody!—I escaped from the Giant's castle…
King What about the Princess?
Mum What about the money?
Olaf He's still got her. But listen—everybody—we can get rid of the Giant once and for all! I've got a plan. I KNOW IT WILL WORK! But we have to move fast! You have to trust me!
Mum But, Olaf, the money…
Dad WILL YOU SHUT UP ABOUT THE MONEY!
King So, Olaf—what's your plan?

Song: A Giant's Giant Pizza Rap

Olaf (*rapping*) The Giant wants a pizza, so this is my plan
We'll give him a pizza not a pudding or a flan
A pizza he'll remember till the end of his days
A pizza to teach him the error of his ways.
We'll make it ten times the size that he stipulates
Ten times the volume and ten times the weight,
The size of a European capital city,
Smelling delicious and looking very pretty.
A pizza any glutton would be proud to own,
Unlike any pizza you can order on the phone
A pizza so amazing and brilliantly inspired
You could gaze at it forever without ever growing tired.
Then comes the best bit of my cunning little plan
King A plan for a pizza not a pudding or a flan.
Olaf We get the pizza baked
Mama Mia Not an easy thing to do
Olaf We'll need a massive oven

Mama Mia	Or maybe even two.
Olaf	Then the doctor comes along with his magic foam
Dr Madcap	Sorry, but I think that I am wanted on the phone. (*He heads towards the exit*)

The Bodyguards stop Dr Madcap from leaving

Olaf	It's vital you deliver to us every single can
King	Fetch the stuff immediately, you'd better take the van.

A couple of Bodyguards rush out with Dr Madcap

Olaf	Then we spread the pizza with the frothy stuff Not too much, or too little, just enough After a while, the foam will take effect The pizza will reduce until it's just perfect.
King	The size the Giant wanted?
Olaf	And a size that we can manage To fly up to his house without it getting damaged.
King	I really like the sound of this, a scintillating plan!
All	A plan for a pizza, not a pudding or a flan!
Mum	Would it make a play, or perhaps even a movie?
Dad	Can we play ourselves in it? That really would be groovy!
Olaf	It's just a question then of him gulping it down Then waiting for the magical foam to get around To losing its power, which takes at most a day, Then the pizza expands in his stomach then, hey! There's a mighty great explosion,
King	And Rumblebottom shatters
Butler	The end of the story!
Olaf	Or all of it that matters!
King	I never heard a plan quite as planish as this Olaf, you're a genius! You deserve a massive kiss!
Olaf	Afterwards, Your Highness we've so much work to do And once we've saved your daughter I'm sure that she'll kiss you
King	Let's do it, everybody! I think we're on a winner And if and when our project works I'll invite you all to dinner! Oh, but I'm forgetting, my bank account is empty…
Olaf	Cash is not a problem, Your Highness, I've got plenty Buy everything's that needed and put it on my bill.

Mum faints

Scene 10

Dad Oh my goodness, Olaf, your mother's taken ill!
Olaf Three cheers for the Princess! Hip hip hip hooray!
King And another three for Olaf, I think he's saved the day!

All exit

Scene 10

The Princess in a giant hot-dog roll. The Giant's shadow on the screen: he's eating a huge pizza. His voice is amplified

Princess Is it good?
Giant Very.
Princess You said you'd let me go when the pizza had been delivered.
Giant I changed my mind.
Princess That's not fair!
Giant When I've finished this, I'm going to eat you, too.
Princess (*after a pause*) I watched some of your videos last night. One of them was really good.
Giant *Beauty and the Beast*? *The Hunchback of Notre Dame*?
Princess No.
Giant *King Kong*? *The Monster From the Deep*?
Princess A home movie of you as a little boy, with your mum and dad, at the seaside. You were all swimming and laughing, and creating new countries by throwing mountains into the sea. (*Pause*) Are you really going to eat me?
Giant If I put plenty of ketchup on you shouldn't taste too disgusting.
Princess You won't have room after all that pizza. It's huge.
Giant So am I.
Princess (*after a pause*) Your dad looked really kind, and your mum. What were their names? Were you an only giant, or did you have brothers and sisters.
Giant None of your business!
Princess There's this really cool bit—your dad's throwing you up in the air, he throws you so high you disappear into the clouds. "Be careful", your mum keeps saying, but you're loving it! You look really, really happy! Do you remember that?
Giant (*after a slight pause*) No.
Princess There's another good bit. You're a baby and you're eating jam tarts, you've got them everywhere, in your hair, round your mouth. Then your dad comes and he takes a jam tart off your head, and eats it! As if it was the most natural thing in the world! What a cool dad! He didn't tell you off or

get angry, just ate the tart! Brilliant! Then he took another one and gave it to your mum. "Thank you", she said! Your folks seemed great. Were they?

Giant (*after a pause*) They were called Oswald and Hilda. Everybody loved them, even the humans, even me. They were always helping people, moving mountains or diverting rivers. At harvest time, my dad would hold his hand up to the sun so that people working in the fields wouldn't get sunburned. "Giants are very lucky", he said to me, once "Because they're so big, even the little things they do help a lot".

Princess Have you finished the pizza?
Giant Yes.
Princess Are you going to eat me, now?

Pause

You are not *really* going to eat me, are you?
Giant Yes! Where did I put the ketchup?

The Giant exits

Olaf appears

Olaf Psst. Princess.
Princess Olaf!
Olaf I've come to get you. (*He frees her from the roll*)
Princess Good timing, Batman!

Olaf puts something in the roll

What's that?
Olaf The Biggest Chilli Dog the World has ever seen! Dressed up to look like you! (*He sprinkles something on to the hot dog*) Extra chilli. He has to drink a lot. To wash off the chemicals. From the foam. On the pizza. If not, it won't grow whilst it's still in his stomach. The pizza. If he drinks the water, it will.
Princess Olaf, what are you babbling about?
Olaf Let's get out of here.

Olaf and the Princess exit

Giant Rumblebottom comes in with a hot dog in a roll

Giant First time I've ever eaten a princess. I wonder what flavour you are? Sugar and spice and all things nice? Ha! Salt and vinegar, more like! At least you've stopped talking—that's something! Well, bye-bye, Princess—

it's been nice knowing you. Not! (*He takes a bite*) Mmm. Wow, this chilli ketchup sure is *hot*! As in—FIRE! HELP! WATER! ARGH!

The Giant rushes out

Scene 11

Outside the Palace of Pizza

Everyone except the Giant on stage, listening intently

Olaf Any moment, now...

Pause, then a rumbling, distant explosion. Everyone sighs with relief and flops down, exhausted

Princess Shame really. He could have been so cute...
Everyone Else Huh?
Princess ...if he hadn't been such a monstrous pig.
Dad Life will be strange without him.
Everyone Huh?!
Dad Who do we blame now for all our misfortunes?
King Olaf—amazing!

All the others variously exclaim "Yeah!", "Absolutely!", "Excellent!", "Brilliant!", "Couldn't have done it better myself!", "Fabulous!", "Well done, Olaf!", "Cool!", "Brill!", "Proper job!", etc.

(*To Mum and Dad*) Your son has saved us all. If not for him, we would have been in the grip of the Giant for ever. I thank you from the bottom of my heart.

Mum Olaf, I must admit I thought you were a complete jerk when you gave all your Lottery winnings away. I still think it's a pity you had to give *all* of it away, but... Well, son, I won't forget this moment as long as I live. I'm so proud! (*She bursts into tears*)

King And now, dinner! Mama Mia, I'm not sure I can face pizza just now, what about some of your excellent spaghetti?

Mama Mia Dinner, it is-a served! (*She ushers everyone inside*) Move-a along! No-a-pushing and a shoving! Plenty food-a for-a every-a-one! Mama Mia! (*Etc. ad lib*)

Olaf and the Princess hang back, then begin to sneak out in the opposite direction. The King comes back out

King Aren't you hungry, Pauline?
Princess Er, well, we thought we'd just take a stroll, first.
King Ah. Yes. Er. Good idea. Why not? Yes! Ha! Right. Well. Mmm. See you later, then. Yes! Ha!

The King goes off

Princess (*astonished*) What, no bodyguards?!
Olaf (*jokily*) It's because he knows you're with me!
Princess No. It's because he knows that, giants apart, (*she floors Olaf with a ju-jitsu throw*) no-one sits on my nose!
Olaf Hey, will you teach me that?

                    Song: Princess Pauline's Song (reprise)
Princess   Olaf, some girls fall in love
                With pictures in a magazine
                They buy all the latest CDs
                Of the lover of their dreams
                They take in all the movies
                Buy all the merchandise
                And moon around each playtime
                With that love-look in their eyes.

As she sings the chorus, the whole Company enter and stand behind Pauline and Olaf

                But Olaf for me there's you
                And Olaf for me you'll do
                Yes Olaf for me there's you
                And I hope that will always be true.

                At school I sit behind you
                So I can watch you secretly
                And it gives me such a thrill
                When I think you might be watching me
                I don't know how it happened
                That I started loving you
                But when you phoned and asked me out tonight
                It was a dream come true.

The whole Company sways in time, singing backing vocals to:

                Because Olaf for me there's you

Scene 11

And Olaf for me you'll do
Yes Olaf for me there's you
And I hope that will always be true. (*Repeat*)

CURTAIN

FURNITURE AND PROPERTY LIST

Further dressing may be added at the director's discretion

Prologue

On stage: Handkerchief

Scene 1

Strike: Handkerchief

Off stage: Sack containing cow, small car, mobile phone (**Giant Rumblebottom**)

Scene 2

On stage: Bucket containing soaking wet balaclava
Sofa

Off stage: Lottery coupons (**Mum**)
Lottery coupons (**Dad**)

Personal: **Olaf:** mobile phone, Lottery tickets

Scene 3

On stage: Sofa

Off stage: Canister of shaving foam (**Nurse**)
Wood-saw (**Nurse**)

Personal: **Dr Madcap :** bill
Olaf: wad of money, watch, balaclava (worn until Scene 9)

Scene 4

Strike: Wood-saw

Furniture and Property List

Off stage: Comic (**Princess**)

Personal: **Butler:** mobile phone
Bodyguards: shades

Scene 5

Strike: Sofa

On stage: Bell
Ladies toilet sign
Stick

Personal: **Olaf:** balaclava

Scene 6

Off stage: Small parachute with box containing miniature pizza (**SM**)
Pizza the size of a wheel (**Princess**)
Rucksack containing cans of spray (**Olaf**)
Miniature Giant (**Olaf**)
Pizza box (**Princess**)

Scene 7

On stage: As before

Scene 8

On stage: As before

Off stage: Burst pizza box (**Olaf**)

Scene 9

On stage: As before

Personal: **Mum:** handbag

Scene 10

On stage: Giant hot-dog roll containing **Princess**
Huge pizza

Off stage: Hot dog in a roll (**Giant Rumblebottom**)

Scene 11

No props

LIGHTING PLOT

Property fittings required: nil
Various interior and exterior settings

PROLOGUE

To open: Overall general lighting

No cues

SCENE 1

To open: Overall general lighting

No cues

SCENE 2

To open: Overall general lighting

No cues

SCENE 3

To open: Overall general lighting

No cues

SCENE 4

To open: Overall general lighting

No cues

Scene 5

To open: Overall general lighting

No cues

Scene 6

To open: Overall general lighting

Cue 1   **Princess**: "Wow—this is something really happening!"   (Page 16)
Light on **Giant** *against backdrop*

Scene 7

To open: Overall general lighting

No cues

Scene 8

To open: Overall general lighting

Cue 2   **Olaf**: "First, my ears—and now, the Giant..."   (Page 20)
Light on **Giant** *against backdrop*

Cue 3   **Giant**: "NO-ONE!"   (Page 21)
Fade light on **Giant**

Scene 9

To open: Overall general lighting

No cues

Scene 10

To open: **Giant**'s shadow on backdrop

No cues

Lighting Plot

SCENE 11

To open: Overall general lighting

No cues

EFFECTS PLOT

Cue 1	To open Scene 4 *Phone rings, continuing*	(Page 8)
Cue 2	**King** answers phone *Cut phone ringing*	(Page 9)
Cue 3	**Princess**: "Just singing and dancing in the…" *Toilet flush*	(Page 13)
Cue 4	To open Scene 6 *Sound of helicopter approaching*	(Page 14)
Cue 5	Small parachute falls to the stage *Fade out helicopter*	(Page 14)
Cue 6	**Olaf** and **Princess** mime spraying foam *Hissing sound of spray*	(Page 16)
Cue 7	To open Scene 8 *Cockerel crows outside*	(Page 19)
Cue 8	**Olaf**: "Any moment, now…" *After a pause, a rumbling, distant explosion*	(Page 27)

www.ingramcontent.com/pod-product-compliance
Lightning Source LLC
Chambersburg PA
CBHW070452050426
42450CB00012B/3248